The Confidence Blueprint:

A Step-by-Step Guide to Building Self-Assurance and Inner Strength

Flawless Dave

Table of Contents

Introduction to Confidence

Definition of confidence

Confidence can be defined as a feeling of self-assurance and belief in one's abilities, qualities, and judgment. It is an essential quality that can help individuals to feel capable and secure in their abilities, and it is an important factor in achieving success in various areas of life.

Confidence is not the same as arrogance or self-importance, which are characterized by an inflated sense of self-worth and a lack of consideration for others. Instead, confidence is about having a realistic belief in one's abilities and an ability to act on them in a respectful and effective manner.

Confidence can be an important factor in many aspects of life, including personal relationships, career advancement, and personal development. It can also help individuals to cope with challenges and setbacks, as it allows them to believe in their ability to overcome obstacles and find solutions.

it is something that can be developed and strengthened over time through positive experiences, self-reflection, and the application of effective strategies and techniques.

The importance of confidence in daily life

Confidence is an important quality that can have a significant impact on an individual's daily life. Some of the ways in which confidence can be important in daily life include:

Self-assurance: Confidence can help individuals to feel self-assured and capable, which can increase their sense of self-worth and self-esteem. This, in turn, can lead to greater happiness and well-being.

Decision-making: Confidence can help individuals to make decisions more easily and effectively, as they are more likely to believe in their own abilities and judgment. This can be important in a variety of situations, including making choices about career, relationships, and personal goals.

Communication: Confidence can also be important in communication, as it can help individuals to speak up for themselves and express their opinions and ideas clearly and effectively. This can be particularly important in work or school settings, where the ability to communicate effectively can be key to success.

Leadership: Confidence can also be an important factor in leadership, as it can help individuals to inspire and motivate others, and to effectively delegate tasks and responsibilities.

The difference between confidence and arrogance

Confidence and arrogance are two distinct qualities that can have very different effects on an individual's behavior and relationships. Some key differences between confidence and arrogance include:

Realistic belief in one's abilities: Confidence is characterized by a realistic belief in one's abilities, qualities, and judgment. It is about feeling self-assured and capable, and it does not involve an inflated sense of self-worth. Arrogance, on the other hand, is characterized by an exaggerated sense of self-importance and a belief that one is superior to others.

Respect for others: Confidence is often accompanied by a respectful and considerate attitude towards others. It does not involve a lack of consideration for the feelings or needs of others. Arrogance, on the other hand, is often characterized by a lack of respect for others and a tendency to put one's own interests above those of others.

Impact on relationships: Confidence can be an attractive quality and can help individuals to build positive relationships with others. Arrogance, on the other hand, can be off-putting and can damage relationships, as it can come across as disrespectful or self-centered.

So, confidence is an important quality that can help individuals to feel self-assured and capable, and it can be an attractive and positive trait. Arrogance, on the other hand, is a negative quality that can damage relationships and create unnecessary conflict.

Understanding the sources of confidence

The role of genetics and personality

Genetics and personality can both play a role in an individual's level of confidence. Here are some ways in which these factors can influence confidence:

Genetics: Research has suggested that genetics may play a role in an individual's level of confidence. Some studies have found that certain personality traits, such as extroversion and openness to experience, may have a genetic basis. These traits are often associated with higher levels of confidencc, and they may be influenced by genetic factors.

Personality: Personality can also influence an individual's level of confidence. Some people are naturally more confident due to their personality traits, such as extroversion, assertiveness, and a tendency towards risk-taking. Others may be more introverted or cautious, which can affect their level of confidence in certain situations.

It is important to note that genetics and personality are just two of many factors that can influence an individual's level of confidence. Other factors, such

as past experiences and upbringing, can also play a role. Additionally, confidence is not a fixed trait and can be developed and strengthened over time through positive experiences and the application of effective strategies and techniques.

The impact of past experiences and upbringing

Past experiences and upbringing can both have a significant impact on an individual's level of confidence. Here are some ways in which these factors can influence confidence:

Past experiences: An individual's past experiences can shape their level of confidence in a number of ways. For example, if someone has had a lot of success in a particular area, they may have a higher level of confidence in their abilities in that area. On the other hand, if someone has had a lot of failures or setbacks, they may have a lower level of confidence in their abilities.

Upbringing: An individual's upbringing can also influence their level of confidence. For example, if someone has been consistently encouraged and supported in their endeavors, they may have a higher level of confidence in their abilities. On the other hand, if someone has been consistently criticized or belittled, they may have a lower level of confidence in their abilities.

It is important to note that past experiences and upbringing are just two of many factors that can influence an individual's level of confidence. Other factors, such as genetics and personality, can also play a role. Additionally, confidence is not a fixed trait and can be developed and strengthened over time through positive experiences and the application of effective strategies and techniques.

The influence of external factors such as appearance and success

External factors, such as appearance and success, can have an influence on an individual's level of confidence. Here are some ways in which these factors can impact confidence:

Appearance: An individual's appearance can influence their level of confidence in a number of ways. For example, if someone is dissatisfied with their appearance, they may have a lower level of confidence in social situations. On the other hand, if someone is happy with their appearance, they may have a higher level of confidence in social situations.

Success: Success can also influence an individual's level of confidence. For example, if someone has had a lot of success in a particular area, they may have a higher level of confidence in their abilities in that area. On the other hand, if someone has had a lot of failures or setbacks, they may have a lower level of confidence in their abilities.

Building self-esteem

The relationship between self-esteem and confidence

Self-esteem and confidence are two related, but distinct, qualities that can influence an individual's thoughts, feelings, and behaviors. Here are some key ways in which self-esteem and confidence are related:

Self-esteem is a person's overall evaluation of their own worth and value as a person. It is an important factor in an individual's level of confidence, as a person with high self-esteem is likely to have a higher level of confidence in their abilities and decision-making. On the other hand, a person with low self-esteem is likely to have a lower level of confidence in their abilities and decision-making.

Confidence is a feeling of self-assurance and belief in one's abilities, qualities, and judgment. It is an important quality that can help individuals to feel capable and secure in their abilities and to navigate the various challenges and opportunities that life presents. Self-esteem can be an important factor in an individual's level of confidence, as a person with high self-esteem is likely to have a higher level of confidence in their abilities.

Self-esteem and confidence can influence each other. For example, if someone has a lot of success in a particular area, it can boost their self-esteem and confidence. On the other hand, if someone has a lot of failures or setbacks, it can lower their self-esteem and confidence.

Self-esteem and confidence are related qualities that can have a significant impact on an individual's thoughts, feelings, and behaviors. While they are distinct qualities, they can influence each other and are both important factors in an individual's overall well-being and success.

Techniques for improving self-esteem, including positive self-talk, self-acceptance, and setting realistic goals

There are a number of techniques that can be effective for improving self-esteem, including:

Positive self-talk: Positive self-talk involves using positive, affirmations to reinforce a positive self-image. This can involve saying things like "I am worthy and capable" or "I am capable of achieving my goals." Positive self-talk can help to counter negative thoughts and beliefs about oneself, and it can help to improve self-esteem.

Self-acceptance: Self-acceptance involves accepting oneself as one is, including both one's strengths and weaknesses. This can involve acknowledging and embracing one's unique qualities and not trying to be someone that one is not. Self-acceptance can help to improve self-esteem, as it allows individuals to feel more comfortable and confident in their own skin.

Setting realistic goals: Setting realistic goals can help to improve self-esteem by providing a sense of accomplishment and progress. When individuals set goals that are achievable and attainable, they are more likely to experience success, which can boost their self-esteem. On the other hand, setting unrealistic goals can lead to disappointment and frustration, which can lower self-esteem.

These techniques can be effective for improving self-esteem, as they help individuals to develop a more positive and realistic view of themselves. This, in turn, can lead to increased confidence and a sense of self-worth.

Overcoming fear and anxiety

Understanding the causes of fear and anxiety

Fear and anxiety can have a negative impact on an individual's confidence by causing them to doubt their abilities and judgment. Here are some ways in which fear and anxiety can dent confidence:

Lack of self-assurance: Fear and anxiety can cause individuals to feel uncertain and unsure of themselves, which can lower their confidence. For example, if someone is anxious about giving a presentation, they may lack confidence in their ability to deliver the presentation effectively.

Negative thoughts: Fear and anxiety can also lead to negative thoughts and beliefs about oneself, which can lower confidence. For example, if someone is anxious about an upcoming test, they may believe that they are not intelligent enough to do well. These negative thoughts can make it difficult for individuals to feel confident in their abilities.

Difficulty taking action: Fear and anxiety can also make it difficult for individuals to take action or make decisions, which can lower confidence. For example, if someone is anxious about trying a new activity, they may be hesitant to give it a try, which

can lower their confidence in their ability to learn new things.

Fear and anxiety can dent confidence by causing individuals to doubt their abilities and judgment, and by making it difficult for them to take action and make decisions. This can make it harder for individuals to feel self-assured and capable, and it can have a negative impact on their overall well-being and success.

Strategies for managing and reducing fear and anxiety, including relaxation techniques, positive visualization, and exposure therapy

There are a number of strategies that can be effective for managing and reducing fear and anxiety, including:

Relaxation techniques: Relaxation techniques, such as deep breathing, progressive muscle relaxation, and mindfulness meditation, can help to reduce anxiety by calming the mind and body.

These techniques can be particularly helpful in reducing anxiety in the short-term, and they can be useful for managing anxiety in the long-term as well.

Positive visualization: Positive visualization involves creating mental images of positive and

successful outcomes in order to reduce anxiety and increase confidence. This can involve visualizing oneself successfully completing a task or achieving a goal. Positive visualization can help to reduce anxiety by providing a sense of control and by allowing individuals to see themselves as capable and successful.

Exposure therapy: Exposure therapy is a type of therapy that involves gradually exposing individuals to the things that they are afraid of or anxious about in a controlled and safe environment. This can help individuals to overcome their fears and reduce their anxiety. Exposure therapy can be an effective treatment for a variety of anxiety disorders, and it can be helpful for reducing anxiety in other areas of life as well.

Developing a growth mindset

The difference between a fixed and growth mindset

A fixed mindset is the belief that one's abilities and characteristics are fixed and cannot be changed, while a growth mindset is the belief that one's abilities and characteristics can be developed and improved through effort and learning. Here are some key differences between fixed and growth mindsets:

Responses to challenges: Individuals with a fixed mindset may view challenges as threats to their abilities and may be more likely to avoid them, while individuals with a growth mindset may view challenges as opportunities for growth and learning.

Responses to failure: Individuals with a fixed mindset may view failure as a sign of their limitations and may be more likely to give up in the face of setbacks, while individuals with a growth mindset may view failure as a learning opportunity and may be more likely to persevere.

Belief in change: Individuals with a fixed mindset may believe that their abilities and characteristics are fixed and cannot be changed, while individuals with a growth mindset may believe that their abilities and characteristics can be developed and improved through effort and learning.

The main difference between a fixed and growth mindset is the belief in the potential for change and improvement. A growth mindset can be an important factor in increasing resilience and adaptability, and it can be developed and strengthened through practice and the application of effective strategies and techniques.

The benefits of a growth mindset, including increased resilience and adaptability

There are a number of benefits to having a growth mindset, including:

Increased resilience: A growth mindset can help individuals to be more resilient in the face of challenges and setbacks. This is because individuals with a growth mindset believe that their abilities can be developed and improved, so they are more likely to persevere and try new approaches when faced with difficulties.

Increased adaptability: A growth mindset can also help individuals to be more adaptable and flexible. This is because individuals with a growth mindset believe that they can learn and grow from new experiences and challenges, so they are more likely to be open to new ideas and approaches.

Improved performance: Research has shown that individuals with a growth mindset tend to have better academic and professional performance than those with a fixed mindset. This is because they are more likely to take on challenges, seek feedback, and learn from their mistakes, which can lead to better outcomes.

Increased well-being: A growth mindset can also be associated with greater well-being, as it allows individuals to see themselves as capable of growth and change, which can increase self-esteem and confidence.

Techniques for developing a growth mindset, including reframing negative thoughts and seeking challenges

There are a number of techniques that can be effective for developing a growth mindset, including:

Reframing negative thoughts: Reframing negative thoughts involves replacing negative beliefs about oneself and one's abilities with more positive and growth-oriented beliefs. For example, instead of

thinking "I'm not good at math," an individual might reframe this thought as "I may not be good at math right now, but I can improve through practice and learning." Reframing negative thoughts can help to develop a growth mindset by shifting the focus from fixed limitations to the potential for growth and improvement.

Seeking challenges: Seeking out new challenges and experiences can also be an effective way to develop a growth mindset. This can involve taking on new tasks or responsibilities, trying new activities, or learning new skills. Seeking challenges can help individuals to see themselves as capable of growth and change, and it can provide opportunities for learning and personal development.

Seeking feedback: Seeking feedback from others can also be an effective way to develop a growth mindset. This can involve asking for feedback on performance, asking for advice on how to improve, or seeking mentorship from someone with more experience. Seeking feedback can help individuals to see their own abilities and limitations more clearly, and it can provide opportunities for growth and learning.

These techniques can be effective for developing a growth mindset, as they help individuals to shift their focus from fixed limitations to the potential for growth and improvement. It is important to note that developing a growth mindset is a process that takes time and practice, and it may be helpful to try a variety of techniques to find what works best for an individual.

Improving communication skills

The importance of effective communication in building confidence

Effective communication is an important factor in building confidence, as it allows individuals to effectively express themselves and assert their needs and desires. Here are some ways in which effective communication can help to build confidence:

Improved self-expression: Effective communication involves being able to express oneself clearly and effectively, which can help individuals to feel more confident in their own thoughts and ideas. When individuals are able to communicate their thoughts and feelings effectively, they are more likely to feel heard and understood, which can boost their confidence.

Improved relationships: Effective communication is also important for building and maintaining positive relationships. When individuals are able to communicate effectively, they are more likely to be able to build trust and understanding with others, which can lead to more positive and fulfilling relationships. This, in turn, can boost confidence by providing a sense of connection and support.

Enhanced problem-solving: Effective communication is also important for problem-solving, as it allows individuals to clearly articulate their needs and concerns, and to listen and understand the perspective of others. This can help individuals to feel more confident in their ability to navigate challenges and find solutions.

Effective communication is an important factor in building confidence, as it allows individuals to effectively express themselves, build positive relationships, and navigate challenges.

Techniques for improving communication skills, including active listening, assertiveness, and body language

There are a number of techniques that can be effective for improving communication skills, including:

Active listening: Active listening involves fully focusing on and engaging with what another person is saying, rather than just waiting for a chance to speak. It involves paying attention to both verbal and nonverbal cues, and it involves demonstrating understanding through verbal and nonverbal responses. Active listening can help to improve communication by allowing individuals to better understand the perspective of others and to build trust and understanding.

Assertiveness: Assertiveness involves expressing one's own needs and desires in an open and direct way, without being aggressive or passive. It involves being able to stand up for oneself and one's beliefs, while also being respectful of the rights and beliefs of others. Assertiveness can help to improve communication by allowing individuals to express themselves effectively and to set boundaries in relationships.

Body language: Body language is an important aspect of communication, and it can have a significant impact on how a message is received. Using positive body language, such as maintaining eye contact, nodding, and using open gestures, can help to convey confidence and engagement, while negative body language, such as crossing one's arms or avoiding eye contact, can convey disinterest or lack of confidence. Being aware of and using positive body language can help to improve communication and build confidence.

They help individuals to better understand the perspective of others, to express themselves effectively, and to convey confidence and engagement through body language. It is important to note that communication skills are complex and multifaceted, and it may be helpful to try a variety of techniques to find what works best for an individual.

Enhancing leadership skills

The connection between leadership and confidence

There is a strong connection between leadership and confidence, as confidence is an important quality for effective leadership. Here are some ways in which confidence can be important for leadership:

Decision-making: Confidence can be important for leadership because it allows leaders to make decisions effectively and with assurance. When leaders are confident in their abilities and judgment, they are more likely to be able to make decisions that are in the best interest of their team or organization.

Communicating vision: Confidence can also be important for leadership because it allows leaders to effectively communicate their vision and goals to their team or organization. When leaders are confident in their vision, they are more likely to be able to inspire and motivate others to work towards common goals.

Leading by example: Confidence is also important for leadership because it allows leaders to lead by example. When leaders are confident in their abilities, they are more likely to be able to set a good example for others to follow.

Confidence is an important quality for effective leadership, as it allows leaders to make decisions effectively, communicate their vision effectively, and lead by example.

Techniques for developing leadership skills, including goal setting, delegation, and problem-solving

There are a number of techniques that can be effective for developing leadership skills, including:

Goal setting: Goal setting involves setting specific, measurable, achievable, relevant, and time-bound (SMART) goals for oneself and one's team or organization. Setting goals can help leaders to focus their efforts, measure progress, and stay motivated.

Delegation: Delegation involves assigning tasks and responsibilities to team members and trusting them to complete them effectively. Delegation can help leaders to build trust and empower their team, and it can also allow leaders to focus on the tasks that are most important for their role.

Problem-solving: Problem-solving is an important leadership skill, as it involves identifying and addressing challenges and issues in a proactive and effective way. Problem-solving can involve gathering information, brainstorming solutions, evaluating options, and implementing a plan of action.

These techniques can be effective for developing leadership skills, as they help leaders to set and work towards goals, empower their team, and address challenges and issues effectively.

Conclusion

Here are the key points that have been discussed so far:

- Confidence is a feeling of self-assurance and belief in one's abilities, qualities, and judgment. It is an important quality that can help individuals to feel capable and secure in their abilities and to navigate the various challenges and opportunities that life presents.
- Self-esteem is a person's overall evaluation of their own worth and value as a person. It is an important factor in an individual's level of confidence, as a person with high self-esteem is likely to have a higher level of confidence in their abilities and decision-making.
- Fear and anxiety can dent confidence by causing individuals to doubt their abilities and judgment, and by making it difficult for them to take action and make decisions.
- There are a number of techniques that can be effective for managing and reducing fear and anxiety, including relaxation techniques, positive visualization, and exposure therapy.

- A fixed mindset is the belief that one's abilities and characteristics are fixed and cannot be changed, while a growth mindset is the belief that one's abilities and characteristics can be developed and improved through effort and learning.

- There are a number of benefits to having a growth mindset, including increased resilience, adaptability, performance, and well-being.
- There are a number of techniques that can be effective for developing a growth mindset, including reframing negative thoughts and seeking challenges.
- Effective communication is an important factor in building confidence, as it allows individuals to effectively express themselves and assert their needs

Building and maintaining confidence is an ongoing process that involves developing and strengthening the skills and qualities that contribute to confidence. Here are some strategies that can be effective for building and maintaining confidence:

Practice self-care: Taking care of one's physical, mental, and emotional well-being is an important

foundation for building and maintaining confidence. This can involve things like getting enough sleep, exercising regularly, eating a healthy diet, and practicing relaxation techniques.

Set and work towards goals: Setting and working towards goals can help to build and maintain confidence by providing a sense of accomplishment and progress. It is important to set realistic and achievable goals, and to celebrate successes along the way.

Seek feedback: Seeking feedback from others can help to build and maintain confidence by providing opportunities for learning and growth. It is important to be open to feedback and to use it as an opportunity to learn and improve.

Practice self-acceptance: Self-acceptance involves accepting oneself as one is, including both one's strengths and weaknesses. This can help to build and maintain confidence by allowing individuals to feel comfortable and confident in their own skin.

Seek out new challenges: Seeking out new challenges and experiences can also be an effective way to build and maintain confidence. This can involve taking on new tasks or responsibilities, trying new activities, or learning new skills.

Also There are a number of ways in which you can apply the concepts and techniques covered in the book to your own lives, depending on the specific material covered in the book. Here are a few general ideas:

Practice the techniques: Many of the concepts and techniques covered in the book may involve specific practices or exercises that readers can try out on their own. For example, you might try out relaxation techniques, positive visualization, or reframing negative thoughts to build confidence and manage anxiety.

Reflect on your own experiences: You are encouraged to reflect on your own experiences and how the concepts and techniques might apply to your own lives can help to make the material more meaningful and relevant to them. This might involve thinking about how you currently respond to challenges and setbacks, or how you currently approach decision-making or communication.

Set and work towards goals: Setting and working towards goals can be an effective way to apply the concepts and techniques covered in the book to one's own life. This might involve setting goals related to building confidence, improving

communication skills, or developing a growth mindset.

Seek out new challenges: Seeking out new challenges and experiences can also be an effective way to apply the concepts and techniques covered in the book to one's own life. This might involve taking on new tasks or responsibilities, trying new activities, or learning new skills.

www.ingramcontent.com/pod-product-compliance
Lightning Source LLC
LaVergne TN
LVHW020536160826
845677LV00015B/4088

* 9 7 9 8 3 7 1 6 0 2 5 2 7 *